The Uses and Abuses of Analysis in the Defense Environment

The Uses and Abuses of Analysis in the Defense Environment

A Conversation with R. James Woolsey

Held on April 2, 1980
at the American Enterprise Institute for Public Policy Research
Washington, D.C.

ISBN 0-8447-3407-1

Library of Congress Catalog Card No. 80-69652

AEI Studies 299

Printed in the United States of America

Introduction

Until recently R. James Woolsey was one of the senior civilians responsible for the overall planning of the U.S. Navy. As the under secretary of the navy, he obviously was responsible directly to the secretary, but he went beyond that very traditional role and became involved in determining the direction the navy should attempt to take on the major issues it faces today.

I say attempt because, as his recent op-ed pieces indicate, seeing problems and seeking solutions are not as simple and as direct as might be assumed. Professor Graham Allison, in his book *The Essence of Decision*, quotes Franklin Roosevelt on that subject. Roosevelt was an assistant secretary of the navy for seven years, from 1913 to 1920—a period of great change in our country. Roosevelt said:

> The Treasury is so large and far-flung and ingrained in its practices that I find it is almost impossible to get the action and results I want. . . . But the Treasury is not to be compared with the State Department. You should go through the experience of trying to get any changes in the thinking, policy, and action of the career diplomats and then you'd know what a real problem was. But the Treasury and the State Department put together are nothing as compared with the Navy. . . . To change anything in the Navy is like punching a feather bed. You punch it with your right and you punch it with your left until you are finally exhausted, and then you find the damn bed just as it was before you started punching.

R. James Woolsey has spent the last three years punching at the feather bed that Roosevelt knew and also at the one in the Department of Defense, which Roosevelt did not know. Thus, he is eminently qualified to discuss the problems of planning the future navy and to give us his estimate on what the real outcome of those plans might be.

WAYNE ARNY
American Enterprise Institute

A Conversation with
R. James Woolsey

I will talk very informally today from the only perspective, or the only position, I could really carve out for myself when I was in the navy secretariat. Playing Andy Devine to the Wild Bill Hickok of Secretary Claytor leaves one only a relatively modest scope for operations. Graham Claytor was the ablest secretary of the navy in some time and will go down in history that way. In trying to find something I could do when I was in that job, I often suggested that I wanted to try to be a party theoretician. That position does not really exist on our side of the iron curtain, but it is one that has always intrigued me. It must have something to do with relating given theory to actual facts and with how one ought to go about thinking about problems one wants to face, at least within the context of the system. The theoretical problem I want to talk about today—how to think about planning the navy's future—does in some degree involve issues similar to those Franklin Roosevelt described. In these days and times, however, the locus of the problem and the quality of resistance of the feather bed are rather different.

For about two decades, the intellectual furniture that has been brought to decision making in the Department of Defense and for the navy, in particular, has been pretty much of one style. With some exceptions, it is a set of intellectual furniture designed about two decades ago in the Office of the Secretary of Defense. Following its acceptance in the Department of Defense, it was accepted throughout much of the rest of the federal government and in many state and local governments, as well. It goes by many names—program analysis or systems analysis, among others. I will call it systems analysis for want of some other term. It is highly quantitative, focused on weapons programs, and rooted in the disciplines of economics and the techniques of business schools. Its primary tenets are to concentrate on objectives, criteria, and options; to quantify as much as possible; and to focus on changes at the margin.

One should assess the systems analysis approach as a method of decision making, quite apart from the individuals who have been involved in it. These have included some extraordinarily able people and some people who have made distinct contributions to the defense debate. But one should ask whether as a method of decision making, it still deserves the allegiance that has been paid to it for nearly two decades now and whether, as a tool of decision making, it may itself involve certain costs and cause certain blind spots.

There have been some excellent academic critiques of the systems approach. Graham Allison, whom Wayne Arny quoted in the introduction, wrote a seminal book, *The Essence of Decision*, which can be viewed as a thorough and decisive critique of the principles behind systems analysis decision making in government. John Steinbruner, now at Brookings and formerly at the Kennedy School at Harvard, and also at Yale, has written widely in this area. But the critiques have not really filtered through into either public discussion or discussion within government.

It is quite possible—and indeed, it happens all the time—for people to develop great allegiances to a certain way of approaching and looking at problems. As a lawyer, I can tell you that lawyers do that. But I would expect lawyers—at least some lawyers—to look at ways to reform, for example, the incredibly cumbersome government regulatory machinery that lawyers have mainly created. It is also fair to ask program analysts or systems analysts to look at themselves and see whether a lot of the diseases in the fields they analyze may not be iatrogenic in nature—that is, unintentionally caused by the physician himself. Just as the problems caused by the complexity of government regulation may not be solved by still more due process in the regulatory system, so the weaknesses associated with program analysis or systems analysis may not be solved best by more analysis. Indeed, we may need considerably less of it.

How has looking at the navy through systems analysts' eyes over the past two decades affected the navy? Let me talk about two main areas—ships and weapon systems, and manpower. With respect to ships and weapon systems, most people would be of the view that systems analysts and the revolution that occurred in defense decision making nearly two decades ago brought rationality to what was then an obsolete system of hunches and biases, dressed up as military judgment, which had reigned through much of the 1950s. The principle was that the defense budget was carved into thirds, and one-third was given to each military department to play around with.

Systems analysis, at its inception, made some important contributions to reforming that system, but the answer to whether it has been a *net* plus has to be both yes and no. My yes is divorced in time from my no. Through some of the 1960s and perhaps even into the 1970s, the answer is yes, but more recently, no would be more accurate.

At first, the reforms that systems analysis brought about were useful in a number of ways. For example, simply looking at the problem from a quantitative point of view forced people to assess whether there was a decent match-up between the logistic structure for the Department of Defense and its force structure—whether we might not have far too little sealift and airlift to get our divisions to a war. In the early days, systems analysis made some very good contributions to that discussion, and it is still making contributions, particularly in that area.

But some rigidity has crept into analysis over the years. The conventional wisdom today within the analytical community would be that the rigidities in navy planning, which continue to exist, are almost entirely attributable to the military conservatism that Franklin Roosevelt mentioned. Especially, the conventional wisdom would point to naval aviators who cling to large aircraft carriers, as if they were some sort of talismanic dinosaurs in the face of efforts by brave and rational analysts to get the admirals to face facts. Recently, the chief of naval operations, Tom Hayward, having been called a dinosaur once too often, responded that dinosaurs after all did rule the world invincibly for several hundred million years and succumbed ultimately only to massive climatic changes. Not many other creatures have matched that record. But quite apart from that point, is this characterization an accurate diagnosis of the source of the navy's problems in looking at the future?

I would submit that it is not. Much of the problem we have with naval planning is iatrogenic, caused by the analytical physicians themselves. Analysts are at least as much involved in sinning as they are sinned against in planning the navy's future. Over the course of the last two decades, planning military forces, particularly for the navy, has become a matter of concocting rather elaborate scenarios for specific geographic areas of the world. These scenarios are boxed in by innumerable assumptions, and force options are created and then tested in the scenarios using complex computer simulations—campaign analyses and the like.

5

Recently, I was involved briefly as an attorney in a prehearing conference before an administrative agency. Dozens and dozens of bright attorneys spent a number of days arguing about the exact content and order of introduction of evidence into a hearing to occur some months later. The interesting question about that sort of hearing and about most scenario-dependent navy force planning, is not "Why don't we do this slightly differently?" but "Why are we doing this *at all?*" One begins to suspect that in some such matters, it is the interests of those who manage the process that are being served, not the illumination of the subject matter. In some cases, that is true for the regulatory system, and it is also true for systems analysis in defense planning.

The studies and the analytical methods themselves have introduced rigidities into the system. At the very least, they often delay and make more difficult the solution of many of the problems they are addressing. At most, they make the problems worse. What has analysis done? Among other things, it has fostered the idea that we can predict the scene and nature of future conflicts, even if we do not plan to be the ones to start them, and that we should not proceed with weapons programs until there are agreements about such scenarios and such analyses. Often, this point is made most petulantly by analysts, more or less along the following lines: "If the damned navy would just decide where and what kind of war it wants to fight, then we could make some progress."

The problem is that the scenarios are a big part of the problem. I do not mean scenarios should not be used, particularly for operational planning—for example, planning how to deploy and use our existing forces. This is the sort of thing that the Joint Chiefs do, what P. X. Kelley is going to be involved in for the Rapid Deployment Force, what the commanders in chief for the Atlantic and Pacific, and others are involved in. But as a tool for designing forces, tools of marginal analysis frequently are themselves useful only in a rather marginal way.

Look at our new Aegis cruisers—the CG47 class that were formerly the DDG47 destroyers. These cruisers are designed to carry a new, very capable air defense system called Aegis, a large phased-array radar that is electronically steered. Aegis will be an extremely important part of battle management for the navy against future generations of cruise missiles or any other aircraft or missile systems that might be involved in an attack on the fleet. Certainly radars, even sophisticated radars of this sort, are no panacea. They will have to be supplemented with other types of sensors. But the CG47 is going to be a very important part of the navy for some time.

We have spent a great deal of time during the years arguing about the exact scenarios in which Aegis might or might not be used. But that is not the only problem. Aegis was delayed by two or three years in getting to sea because the House and the Senate disagreed in the early 1970s whether Aegis ought to be on ships propelled by gas turbines or on ships propelled by nuclear reactors. Setting that two- or three-year delay aside, many other delays have occurred since the system was originally conceived some time in the late 1950s or early 1960s. I would submit that the debate and discussion about analytical problems have been responsible for part of that delay. Some analysts have said, and would say today, that we should go slowly with Aegis, or hold it up, until the scenarios are clearer. They would say that if the navy would just stop trying to design forces to sail up quite close to the Soviet Union—within range of their land-based aircraft—we would not need these elaborate systems at all, or at least not in any great numbers.

The problem is severalfold. First of all, we have several allies—Norway, Turkey, Japan, and others—that have the misfortune to be situated rather close to the Soviet Union. It would not be in either their or our best interests for us to design our forces on the assumption that they are to be behind enemy lines in the next conflict. Second, while we have been haggling about the realistic nature of various scenarios, the Soviets have been making the dispute not altogether irrelevant, but far less relevant, by designing and building the Backfire bomber. It has been assigned in rather large numbers to Soviet naval aviation. Because of its great range, it brings many of the world's ocean areas within range of Soviet land-based aircraft. This includes virtually all of the Atlantic down to about the Azores, all of the Mediterranean, all of the Northern Indian Ocean, and all of the Pacific from about 100 to 200 miles northwest of Pearl Harbor on to Japan. So Aegis would be needed in wartime to cope with cruise missiles or with other missiles that might be launched by Backfire bombers operating in these regions of the world, regardless of whether we plan to try to operate quite close to the Soviet Union.

This realization has produced further analytical dialogues in which analysts from time to time attempt to show how, in a conflict against the Soviet Union, we might avoid sending naval forces into many of *these* regions of the world—the North Atlantic, the Mediterranean, and so forth. This sort of dialogue actually takes place; it is very much part of the decision-making mechanism. The point is that we do not need continuous haggling about scenarios; we need to try to figure out how to make weapons platforms relatively insensitive to technological change. The truth is that we do not really know where or when we are going to have to fight. The lead time for weapons design and production is vastly greater than our ability to forecast where war might occur or even what countries, such as Iran, might or might not be on our side.

Instead of clinging to our fascination for forecasting, we ought to change the way we design and produce weapon systems. Today, we design a weapon system, such as Aegis, and then design a ship around it. This process, even if analysis or congressional debate proceeds expeditiously, sometimes can take a decade or more. Ships can last, with service-life extension programs, forty years or so. *Midway*, which just returned from the Indian Ocean, is three years younger than the recently retired under secretary of the navy. *Midway*'s keel was laid in the middle of war with Japan; she is now home-ported in Japan. Her design has been maintained as a contemporary one. The reason is not so much that we forecasted accurately in 1944, when we laid her keel, the scenarios in which *Midway* might have to serve. It is because she and other carriers can take many changes of generations of aircraft with only minor ship modification. That has meant that *Midway*'s mission could change six, seven, eight times since she first went into service right after World War II.

We need to concentrate on how we can make other weapon systems and platforms as friendly to technical change as aircraft carriers are. Today, that is not possible with surface ships to any very great extent. It is difficult with submarines except insofar as sensors and torpedos change. One important thing to focus on is how to move to more modular construction—not so much for the ships themselves, but for the weapon systems for ships—so that different weapons and sensors may be fitted onto different ships and changed relatively readily. The key to doing this is handling the electronics in a rather different manner than it is handled today. The miracles the American electronics industry has wrought with microminiaturization, chips, and so on, make it possible to have more distributed signal processing for weapon systems. Essentially, each weapon or sensor could do virtually all of its thinking for itself, so that the ship's electronics need not be designed around a single central computer. Those sorts of changes can make possible modernization of ships or other platforms—even tanks and aircraft—in ways that would allow their sensors and weapons to keep pace with technological change far more quickly than they can at the present time. But that is not the sort of problem or the sort of solution on which analysis, as it is normally practiced, focuses our attention.

8

Quite apart from things of such grand scope, such as changing the method of ship, weapon, and sensor construction, one can make some other judgments with respect to naval force planning without going through extremely elaborate scenario-dependent analytical calculations. For example, over the long run it is likely that the role of the attack submarine, whether nuclear-powered or diesel-powered, is going to be terribly important. The advent of the cruise missile, which can be placed on submarines and launched from under water, has meant that submarines are likely to serve an increasingly varied role in all sorts of naval warfare in the future, even more than they do today. When we are laying down one attack submarine a year and the Soviet Union is laying down an average of one every five weeks, one might surmise that something is wrong. In the immortal words of Bob Dylan, who has been quoted in other contexts, "You don't need a weatherman to know which way the wind blows."

The second major point I want to make about analysis is that it has tended to lay down analytical categories that I call intellectual moraines. As the national-security-debate glacier moves through Washington and other cities, it tends to pick up refuse and lay it down in patterns that appear to be purposeful. I am not quite sure what moraines resemble—fences, roads—but they are really just lines of rocks.

The analytical debate has operated like a glacier in that regard. It has at various times in the past laid down such categories as "projection," "sea control," and "presence," which have very little to do with the way anyone actually plans naval forces. "Sea control" essentially meant, in the late 1960s and early 1970s, that we had spent too much time and effort on naval fighter and attack aviation and that we needed to focus on the Soviet submarine threat. "Presence" is not a force-planning objective at all; it is a description of what to do with forces we already have. I cannot imagine any of the great figures of naval history—Drake, Nelson, Mahan, Nimitz— wanting to design a navy for purposes of being present somewhere. But studies get written and people actually carry on debates and discussions about which forces we should buy for purposes of being present somewhere, as if the whole issue of what the navy is for— that is, to be able to engage successfully in combat—could be conveniently set aside and the discussion confined within one of those moraines.

What one wants to emphasize in designing naval forces, or any other type of military forces, is what one wants to destroy. War is about destruction. That is an unpleasant fact, but it is one that should be kept continually in front of people's minds. Part of the problem is that we have tended to talk in terms of management and economics so much that we have let categories like presence loom up and distract our attention from the essence of planning for war, which is planning for destruction.

Jim Stockdale is a retired vice admiral, extraordinary test pilot, extraordinary combat hero, Medal of Honor winner, one of the highest-ranking prisoners of war in Vietnam, and man of letters of some note. A short time ago, Stockdale wrote, "War is a unique human enterprise that cannot be managed on the margin. Clausewitz wrote, 'War is a special profession, however general its relation may be, and even if all the male population of the country capable of bearing arms were able to practice it, war would still continue to be different and separate from any other activity which occupies the life of man.' Contrast this," Stockdale writes, "with a paragraph from a 1974 study entitled *U.S. Tactical Air Power*, 'Waging war is no different in principle from any other resource transformation process and should be just as eligible for the improvements in proficiency that have accrued elsewhere from technical substitution.' " Stockdale continues:

> This is simply not true. There are men who in battle can realize proficiency that would be labeled impossible by any systems analyst, men who make two plus two equal five time after time, on the basis of their personal courage, leadership, strength, loyalty, and comradeship. When the chips are down and you're facing real uncertainty instead of that on a projected profit and loss sheet, you need something more than rationalist stuffing. The first step is to acknowledge that fighting men resent being manipulated by carrot and stick enticements. They have no solace in being part of some systematic resource transformation process when they're told to go harm's way. In short, you can't program men to their deaths, they have to be led.

Force planning, although it does have some differences, is more like what Jim Stockdale was discussing, which is fighting a war, than it is like many "resource transformation processes." A planning process that focuses on what one wants to destroy, what portions of the enemy forces—for example, anti-submarine-warfare, anti-surface-warfare, anti-air-warfare, or the destruction of targets on land—is a far more reasonable way to structure most force-planning problems than is the litany of projection, sea control, presence, crisis management, and the other terms used in the analytical community.

Several thousand years ago, the Chinese philosopher and writer Sun Tzu wrote that there are four ways to defeat an enemy. The least desirable is to destroy the bodies of his soldiers or people, because that is very difficult. Next is to destroy his logistics; that is still difficult. Better is to destroy his alliances. But best of all is to destroy his strategy. Essentially, what that means is destroying the mind of the enemy commander. Analysis, as it works today in the defense community, does not really focus on destroying enemy commanders' minds.

The third problem is not merely that analysis, if done with different categories or if done a different way, might make yet greater contributions. It is that we need a great deal more synthesis and a good deal less analysis. Program analysts tend to focus on programs. They will, as most of us will, round up the usual suspects each year, dust off last year's study, and put together a memorandum that compares and contrasts the relative merits of, let's say, CG47 cruisers to FFG frigates. They will suggest buying a few more of one or a few fewer of the others. This is basically a silly way to approach the problem. True, CG47s and frigates are both surface ships, but they have quite different roles. One is primarily an anti-air-warfare system; the other is primarily an anti-submarine-warfare system. Analyzing them together, comparing and contrasting them, deciding to buy a few more of one and a few less of the others, is not quite as silly, but almost as silly, as having a government office in charge of delivery programs analyze trade-offs between funds for obstetrics wards and funds for post offices.

The main problem, after we assess optimal ways of destroying specific parts of enemy forces, is to try to figure out how to integrate our own forces. An anti-submarine-warfare problem in modern naval warfare becomes an anti-air-warfare problem in a split second if the submarine launches a cruise missile. The great need for the future—especially in light of the Soviet expansion into overseas bases—is going to be integrated fleets that are able to fight in several environments at once, above the surface of the water, on it, underneath it, and against land targets. A large number of problems are going to be centered on command, control, and communications, on substituting one sensor for another (sometimes in a split second), and on using in different and innovative ways platforms that were primarily designed for one purpose—for example, using attack submarines equipped with conventional-warhead cruise missiles to attack land targets without using nuclear warheads. Program-by-program analysis, as it is normally practiced, has almost nothing to say about issues of synthesis and integration, any more than it does about ways to make the navy more readily modernizable or about destroying the enemy's mind.

So much for weapons. How about manpower? Virtually everyone who deals with military manpower questions today in government in one way or another comes at them from the perspective of program analysis. In this context, the tenets of analyzing military manpower questions are that military manpower is a commodity, like labor in the civilian labor market, and that it essentially can be purchased on the market. I want to stress here that I am not referring to the debate between the all-volunteer force and the draft, which sometimes gets mixed up with this issue. That is a much more complicated philosophical matter involving libertarianism and many other issues associated with it. The suggestions I am about to make in no way imply that one needs necessarily to abandon the all-volunteer force for a selective service system.

Most of the people who analyze military manpower questions do not regard it as important to assess such issues as the motivation of people in the military. They believe that service in military organizations can be reduced to a fee-for-service basis. One feature of this is a heavy reliance on bonuses and other incentives, focused on precise problem points, such as the end of the first enlistment, when a large number of people leave the armed services. Another feature is a great suspicion in the analytical community toward providing any payments in kind, such as subsidized commissaries or post exchanges or educational benefits. Sailors, according to the analytical assumptions, are economic men like everyone else; they have normal discount rates. Pay them in cash, and if they want to save it and go to college, they can. That is their business. The market will handle the problem.

This attitude, this complex of views, tends to produce a certain blindness to such issues as what social class people are coming from when they go into the military. What about their taste for, and interest in, upward mobility? What are their motivations? Those issues receive attention only if they can be reduced to some particular quantitative measure, such as the percentage of high school graduates being brought into the armed forces. Such measurements may fit easily into a computer model, but often not too much attention is paid to their real worth—for example, the worth of focusing on high school graduate percentages as an indicator of actual quality in armed forces.

What has been the result? Today, the navy is about 20,000 petty officers short. It is not only the primary problem in navy manpower or in navy readiness, in the judgment of the chief of naval operations, it is also the primary problem for the navy, period. He has held his breath, bitten his tongue, and said that he would give up shipbuilding money to retain his petty officers if the administration and Congress would let him do it. The shortages of noncommissioned officers, petty officers, mean that more than eighty ships now out with the fleet are not fully ready for combat. Such manpower shortages have produced a syndrome. There must be more inspections because the officers cannot be certain that the petty officers are seeing to it that equipment and weapons are being maintained in proper order; everyone has to work longer hours; and morale goes down. All those factors feed upon one another.

Solutions to those problems are vital. I fully agree with former Secretary Laird's statements in his recent AEI paper that a pay raise is needed, especially for career military personnel. Their salaries have fallen about 15 percent or so below the inflation rate since the all-volunteer force was introduced in 1972. But noncommissioned officers in the military also become upset at a number of things besides pay levels. One is the constant fiddling with benefits of various sorts—commissaries, retirement, reductions here, changes there. They feel that the life they have chosen and the terms of that life have no permanence or stability. They are extremely upset about being sent untrainable recruits.

Parenthetically, I used to correct the chief petty officers on that point. I said I agreed with them on many things, but if they would just look at the statistics, they would see that the people coming into the military under the all-volunteer force today were on the average considerably brighter than those entering under the peacetime draft. I basically dismissed what they were saying about being sent untrainable recruits as standard military complaining. A few weeks ago, the Defense Department revealed that for some years its statistics have been wildly off regarding the intelligence levels of recruits. They are now doing some studies to get it straight, but instead of 5 percent or so of those people who enter the armed forces being considerably below average in intelligence—the so-called category IV—the percentage is probably closer to 25 percent. That is the last time I am going to believe a computer before I believe a chief petty officer.

The thrust of these complaints—the constant fiddling around with benefits, sending untrainable recruits, and so on—is that the administration and Congress do not seem to care anymore. A programmatic focus, a quantitative focus, a heavily cost-focused analysis of military manpower problems for the navy and the other services has drawn attention *away* from the navy and the other services as institutions. Ed Yoder, the head of the editorial page of the *Washington Star*, gave an extraordinary lecture at the University of North Carolina a few weeks ago, reprinted in the *Star* on a recent Sunday. It focuses on exactly this kind of problem—a lack of concern with institutions in contemporary American life. Outside the military, nobody has been looking hard at such questions as: What motivates people to stay in the military? How do they feel about their own personal security? How do the constant moves and family separation affect them? How does it happen that we are not able anymore to attract enough people to grow into good noncommissioned officers? What motivates people to be upwardly mobile? How does this tie in with job performance? What role might education benefits have in attracting people who are motivated in this way? These are important questions. The fact that they are not on most program analysts' or systems analysts' agendas or on their normal turf does not mean the questions are any less important.

In summary, the intellectual tradition that has produced program analysis and systems analysis, is an important one. It is a tradition reaching back probably before, but certainly to, Locke, Mill, Adam Smith, Ricardo, and the roots of modern economics. But that tradition may not have cornered the market on reality. Other traditions are relevant, too. The manpower area, for example, those traditions identified with Edmund Burke and his perspective on institutions as resembling organisms more than machines, might have something to say to us. Institutions not only need to be managed, they also need to be held in trust. In the weapons area also, the traditions of economics are not the be-all and end-all of assessing military worth. The tradition that used to be called strategy, reaching back at least to Sun Tzu, is an important one, and one that deserves more attention.

This has all been very heavy. I am not trying to offer any single solution to the navy's or the military's problems. Analysts, as individuals, may well make some further important contributions as many have already. Many are very wise and bright people. But as keepers of a supposedly neutral and comprehensive mechanism for assessing and balancing all of the relevant factors for decision making about defense, as priests of this new faith that breezed into town nearly two decades ago, my suggestion to the analytical community would be the same as that made by Oliver Cromwell to the Long Parliament: "You have sat too long in that place for any good that you may be doing. Go and let us have done with you. Go. In the name of God, go."

Questions and Answers

Murray L. Weidenbaum, American Enterprise Institute: As a former systems analyst in the defense industry, who took your advice and went, it strikes me that what you say is both cogent and, unfortunately, to be expected. When Charlie Hitch and his crew from Rand first joined the Department of Defense, in about 1961, they represented a burst of creative analysis. Now, in that second negative phase you describe, the bureaucrats are taking over. The thrust of your criticism is toward the core of systematic analysis, step one, which is the most difficult and the most time-consuming part of the process—that is, stepping back from the details of the weapons systems and truly analyzing the system of national defense. But the bureaucrats who are doing the individual systems analyses are not expected each time to replicate that overall systems analysis, and that is where the problem really lies. You have given me a very convincing argument, not for eliminating systems analysis, but for taking a very new look, no doubt with new people, at how to do that essential step of systematic analysis that Hitch and company did in 1961 and that cries for doing in the light of the 1980s.

Mr. Woolsey: I would agree. A number of the people associated with the analytical community during the years, including some who are right now at the top of it, are extraordinarily able people who have made a great contribution to the defense debate. What I object to is their acting as both counsels for the plaintiff and court clerks— both players and referees. I would be delighted if they were just counsels for the plaintiff, because many issues with respect to defense policies should be challenged and challenged vigorously. What I have a problem with is having that clash occur, and then having the fellow who is involved in sorting out the issues for the judge be the same fellow who has been representing one of the litigants.

Robert Pranger, American Enterprise Institute: I would agree with you, but using the Stockdale quotation is a little bit unfair, particularly if you put it in the context of hero and the like. I do not know if he was downed by a surface-to-air missile (SAM) in Vietnam, but if he was, this is a very ironic statement.

Mr. Woolsey: I think he was shot down by anti-aircraft gunfire (AAA).

15

MR. PRANGER: Okay, AAA. In flying against SAM systems, of course, two plus two does equal four—that is a technological revolution the Soviets are also aware of, just as targeting and ICBM corresponds to the laws of physics. The ICBM does not need some Air Force officer on board, as in *Dr. Strangelove*, to guide the missile down. It is either there, or it is not. So, defense obviously requires an enormous amount of pure mathematics, which is two plus two equals four. But a good deal of experience in Vietnam among those glorious leaders out of the military academies and others has shown that two plus two often equals minus five. In Vietnam, the shape of the armed forces under the draft was such that we got virtually nothing out of input. Sometimes, two plus two equals five, but if we put the planning perspective of the Department of Defense into the Stockdale framework, as beyond two plus two equals four, it is pretty much standard service academy talk. It just is not the real world.

MR. WOOLSEY: It may be no less valuable for being standard service academy talk. I would be the first to agree that one cannot repeal the principles of physics and that science and technology have a great impact on our ability to fight successfully and that they did so in Vietnam. I would suggest two things, however. First of all, Vietnam, as almost no other war we have fought, is a particularly good example of a war fought according to the principles of marginal analysis. The actual tactics used in Vietnam—a little more of this, slightly more bombing here, try and see, and so forth—are normally identified far more with the civilian marginal approach toward things than they are with the military man's instinct for the jugular. For better or for worse, Vietnam was not exactly fought the way in which most of the military people who were involved in it were actually recommending that it be fought.

The other thing I would suggest is that the chemistry that makes us able to use technology successfully is frequently one that requires judgment, strategy, and a sense of how to integrate a number of factors in ways not really promoted by systems analysis. For example, I believe it is true that Guderian was outnumbered on the western front by the French and British in tanks, and he did not possess armor radically better in technology than theirs. One of his greatest insights was tactical. It was made possible because he outfitted tanks with radios so that he could deploy them in radically different ways than they had been deployed in the past (by simple flag signals and so forth). Guderian was in a part a communicator by profession as a result of some of his early military service. Two plus two equaled four in the sense that he had to know how radios work and that they could work in tanks. But his insight was not a scientific insight. The insight that made the blitzkrieg possible was far more the sort of insight that Sun Tzu talked about than one that a systems analyst would tend to talk about.

JAMES C. MILLER III, American Enterprise Institute: I agree with a lot you say, and I am something of an amateur observer of all these issues. I want to comment on two. You mentioned earlier that perhaps, just like lawyers need to take a look at regulation, economists need to take a look at systems analysis. For most of us who are students of regulation, the very last people we would want to address the problems are the attorneys. They always come up with the wrong solutions, and that also probably would be true in the case of problems with systems analysis.

The question of incentives is of interest, not only for the individual fighting man or woman, but also in terms of something that is almost implicit in an editorial you wrote—that is, the technological revolution. About ten years ago, with several of my graduate school student colleagues, I edited a book on the volunteer army. In it we quoted H. Von Thunen, who is an economist. In 1875, he said, "For here one will sacrifice and battle a hundred human beings in the prime of their lives without a thought in order to save one gun. The reason is that the purchase of a cannon causes an outlay of public funds, whereas human beings are to be had for nothing by means of a mere conscription decree." This suggests that the set of incentives, the set of relative costs for different kinds of inputs, is a very important way of engaging the appropriate structure for a defense— the way we go about defending the nation or assume an aggressive posture.

MR. WOOLSEY: I completely agree with that. We want to put very high value on the lives of our people and our soldiers, particularly our trained soldiers. My problem is not the one you mention on the military manpower side, even within the context of maintaining an all-volunteer force (which has certain attractive features to it). In doing any kind of calculation about how best to balance people and hardware in military forces, we have been captivated by the quantitative and by reducing everything to a fungible entity like dollar cost, which we can put into a computer and use for studies. We have not looked nearly enough at questions like motivation, which Charlie Moskos, the sociologist from Northwestern, examines. With a broader view of what people are all about and what causes them to do things than is normally taken in these analytical studies, we might find ways to maintain an all-volunteer force. Further, that may be the only way we are going to be able to save the all-volunteer force and avoid going back to conscription. But I have no difficulty with what you said.

THOMAS F. JOHNSON, American Enterprise Institute: As I understand it, the problem the military has now is doing just what you said—keeping people in the service long enough for them to be of some use to the service. It is not that we need to build up a level of manpower much above what we have but that we need to be able to retain beyond the first enlistment and beyond, say, the first four or five years for officers, so that they will be the core we can depend on in the future.

MR. WOOLSEY: Broadly speaking, that is true. But I would add two footnotes. One is that we are doing better today than at many times in the past in retaining people past the first enlistment. We have put the vast majority of the incentives—being able to select your next assignment, bonuses, and so forth—at that decision point, the end of the first enlistment. We are not doing too badly there compared with the past.

What is not working out well at all is retaining people at the end of their second enlistment. Roughly speaking, for example, the navy ought to retain something close to two-thirds of the people who reach the end of their second enlistment, but we are not even retaining half. That is what primarily creates that petty-officer gap I described. It used to be the case that if we got people to the end of their first enlistment and then were able to get them to reenlist, the odds were very, very high that they would make the military their career. That is not happening anymore, at least not in the numbers that it needs to happen. Some of the things I was talking about—indifference to the institution and family separation—are important parts of the reason we do not retain those people who reach the end of their second enlistment.

A few months ago, I probably would have agreed that the first-term problem was not all that severe. By first-term problem, I mean initially attracting people into the military. Indeed, for the first four months of fiscal 1980, recruiting is up to about 98 or 99 percent of the totals for all of the services in the aggregate. But the real question now, particularly in light of these new Defense Department statistics, is, What kind of people are we getting? Are we getting people who—even though they may be high school graduates and may be able to sit at a desk for several years and not cause any particular problem—are so low on the intelligence scale and so passive that they are not able to learn to go through the several-step firing sequence to fire a simple shoulder-held infrared anti-aircraft weapon or to recognize aircraft silhouettes? So a problem exists with the people initially coming in, and it is more severe than anyone recognized up until a month or two ago.

MICKEY D. LEVY, American Enterprise Institute: I have some problems with what you say about working on the margins, specifically with regard to the Vietnam war. Economists and businessmen work on the margin in terms of some function—that is, businessmen maximize profits, and profit is a function. One of the failures of program analysts or policy analysts in the defense area is a failure to identify at the outset some objective functions. I understand that is very difficult and that it requires working with some of the heads of departments and the political decision makers. But it seems that policy analysts cannot really do their jobs until they have identifiable objective functions, against which they can analyze how best to achieve various goals.

MR. WOOLSEY: I would say two things about that. First, in one sense, marginal analysis just means ignoring sunk costs. It is, therefore, the first principle of all successful poker players and probably most successful businessmen. In that sense of the meaning, I have no problem with focusing on the margin. But I am not quite sure what you mean by the objective function a program analyst must have. Would destroying the mind of an enemy commander be an objective function?

MR. LEVY: I do not know. You seem to be saying that in the Vietnam war working on the margin may have hurt, but to me there is just no objective function at all. How is the policy analyst supposed to go about analyzing on a nonpartisan basis the most efficient way to do a job if he does not know what he is trying to match?

MR. WOOLSEY: Do you mean by "no objective function" that we did not know what the hell we were trying to do?

MR. MILLER: Some rather important constraints also existed during that period, which we must characterize as political. The analyst knew that troops could not go past the demilitarized zone—they could not do this, they could not do that.

19

MR. LEVY: What I am saying is it is not only a failure of the program analyst, it also seems to be the failure of the head of the analysis division to sit down with the decision makers and say, "Okay, what are our objectives? Are they to wipe out the enemy, are they presence or what?" Then the analysts would have some idea of how and where to begin.

MR. WOOLSEY: I do not by any means want to lay the responsibility for the failure of the Vietnam war at the feet of the systems analysts. Many of them did yeoman service, particularly in assessing things like the logistics structure for Vietnam. I said that in the context of a riposte to Mr. Pranger on the question of whether Stockdale's comment—that a resource transformation process is not the proper model to use in terms of fighting—was or was not a useful way of looking at the problem. My suggestion is that Stockdale is right; it is not a very useful way to look at the problem of fighting.

As Mr. Pranger said, we obviously need to understand that the principles of physics cannot be repealed, and that the military business is a very technical business. But I would add that the "glasses" systems analysts wear have a certain filter that tends to lead them into having an instinct for the capillaries. They look for just a few more of these or a few less of those and say that the main problem we need to concentrate on is the main thing our models tell us we can study. It is like the joke about the drunk under the street light. "Why are you on your hands and knees under the streetlight?" "I'm looking for my car keys." "Is that where you lost them?" "No." "Then why are you there?" "Because this is the only place there's any light." It is that kind of problem. If the keys really *are* under the streetlight, it would be fine to look for them there. I think that would be perfectly all right.

MR. MILLER: Mr. Woolsey raised another issue about conscript forces and analyzing costs. I can virtually guarantee that under the all-volunteer program the Vietnam war would not have lasted ten years or whatever and would not have escalated to 500,000 people in the field. The reason is that we would not have been paying people $120 a month or whatever. We would have to sustain them at the all-volunteer wage. Cost would then become a major calculation and would, in essence, affect the objectives of the war. The fact is that the war objectives in Vietnam were in no way determined by resource transfer, but by seat-of-the-pants notions, which changed during the course of the war. People were relying on a factor of manpower, which was not really a calculation, except in terms of the so-called body count. That is not a systems analysis approach to anything. It is not a rational calculation. Systems analysis may have dressed up aspects of that war, but that war was not fought in terms of any cost-benefit analysis. McNamara's only handle on personnel costs in the war was the body count. I thought the all-volunteer force was an effort to get a handle on costs in terms other than just sheer bodies. That was not a war fought on the basis of systems analysis, and systems analysis should not take the rap.

MR. WOOLSEY: There are two things to be said about that. One is that no war is going to be fought using an all-volunteer force, and no one has contended that it will be. The all-volunteer force is a peacetime system, and anybody who even remotely imagines that we would be in a real war for more than a few weeks and maintain the all-volunteer force is dreaming. That is what the entire debate is about with respect to peacetime registration for the draft. We, or some other country, might be able to fight a war of about the length and intensity of the Yom Kippur War in 1973 without going to conscription or some other type of mobilization of manpower.

MR. PRANGER: But you are going to have to fight the war on all-volunteer salaries, and that in itself is going to be a constraint even if you draft.

MR. WOOLSEY: I completely agree with that.

MR. MILLER: Consider the first time we left the volunteer army. The first conscription was during what we Southerners characterize as the War between the States. In that war, Union forces were manned by less than 2 percent conscripts. I do not know that much about the First World War, but in the Second World War, at least initially, the role of the draft was simply to queue up the volunteers. We all hope and pray that we do not have to fight that kind of war, but war involving large masses of manpower probably would not be socially acceptable today unless we were in a dire crisis, even if we returned to the draft. In regard to what we perceive to be a lot of the social costs of the Vietnam war, the single thing we could do that would relieve more tension than anything else in this country is to eliminate the draft. Those lessons should not be forgotten.

MR. WOOLSEY: Insofar as those comments suggest that we would be able to fight a war of more than a few weeks without returning to some kind of conscription, I just disagree. Insofar as you and Mr.

Pranger are saying that the existence of the draft probably made it easier for national decision makers to get involved in Vietnam, you may well be right. But I do not think that point has anything in particular to do with the comment that started all this, which is whether Vietnam was fought along the principles of systems analysis, marginal analysis, or what have you. I would submit that Stockdale's comments in that regard are well taken. Systems analysts did not run the war, but it is true that at least some military people made recommendations like the one Ridgway, for example, made in 1954 about Vietnam: "Either you're going to have to get all the way in with half a million people or you're not going to be able to do anything. Fish or cut bait." I do not recall those sorts of recommendations in Vietnam, or in the Vietnam era, coming from the systems analysts. They may not have come as much as they should have from the military either. But the approach of a little bit more of this might work, a little bit more of that might work, a highly quantitative assessment of results with respect to trucks on the Ho Chi Minh trail, and all of that has at least certain family resemblances to the force-planning approach that I was attempting to critique. I will not claim any more for it than that.

ROBERT A. GOLDWIN, American Enterprise Institute: You will probably be interested in an AEI publication entitled *Bureaucrats, Policy Analysts, and Statemen—Who Leads?* It is not about the military but about the uses and influence of policy analysts throughout government. That is also the question here. What is the proper role and use of policy analysis? It is easy to criticize the results, if the systems analysts are left to ask the questions or decide what questions ought to be asked. If that happens, it is somebody else's failure.

MR. WOOLSEY: Agreed. But over the course of the last couple of decades, a very high proportion of the people in government who are interested in these kinds of issues have come from, or at least passed through, the analytical community. One picks up certain intellectual furniture in making that journey. Certainly, other people are around, but what I am trying to describe is not so much a failure or a problem with any individual cabinet member, president, or administration, but rather a way of looking at the problem of national security. This approach has achieved a great deal of currency in the academic world, in various institutions, and throughout the government, and I think it needs a good deal of shaking up.

MR. WEIDENBAUM: Much of your concern relates to what seems to be lousy systems analysis, like in the manpower area. It would be a fine econometrician but a lousy economist who would look at the manpower question in terms of the pay structure it will take to optimize the military's retention of its manpower. A good systems analyst would start with a very fundamental question—Why are people leaving? But I do not read that in most of the critiques. The analysts do not seem to raise the question. If they did, then they could weigh alternative ways of dealing with that.

Mr. Woolsey: I completely agree with that. I forget when it was—probably in the late 1940s at some point—that Albert Wohlsteter was asked the question, Where should the B-47s be based in Europe? He did an analytical study, and the answer that came back was, take them out of Europe. That is good systems analysis. That is arguing with the question. The problem is that all too frequently that is not done, and it is so often not done that one begins to wonder whether it is wise to rely so heavily on the discipline if we can only get consistently good work out of people like Albert Wohlsteter.

Mr. Pranger: Of course you know what Melvin Laird's response to that is, and apparently the Senate is backing him. He would say that first we must get the military pay up to the point the Gates Commission promised in the first place. Then, we can look for other answers, because right now a basic living wage just is not there.

Mr. Woolsey: That is certainly justified for the career force. With respect to the first-termers, however, some of the educational benefits might deserve a closer look.

Thelma Lavine, American Enterprise Institute: I find your critique of systems analysis and the entire logic of the argument very commendable, but I would like to make these two points. You criticized systems analysis first of all with regard to weapons, and your criticism of it was its failure, with its hang-up on scenarios, to deal with specific weapons that would transcend shifting scenarios. Second, when you came to manpower, you were criticizing systems analysis on quite different grounds—namely, on quantitative grounds and on the failure of systems analysis to be concerned with motivation, with human nature, or with the concern for institutions.

I am not sure I see how these two come together, and I wonder whether, in effect, you are offering two kinds of criticisms of systems analysis. When you conclude very effectively and dramatically that systems analysis should go, are you saying it should totally go, or are you saying that it should be improved along the lines of your first criticism dealing with weapons? If it is the latter case, are you arguing for some kind of new methodology that would take its place, and is that to be then a mixed methodology, namely, quantitative and qualitative? Or is it going to be totally qualitative? But you have not argued that it should be. Of course my main point with regard to the first case is that systems analysis will not go away unless there is some cogent, appealing methodology to take its place.

Mr. Woolsey: Superb question. I have not tried to suggest any single, integrated solution to what I regard as the failings of analysis. I do not think one exists. No very good replacement exists for exercising good judgment, attracting good people into government, and trusting them to do a good job. I would like to see more people in the game with what, for reasons of shorthand, I will call a Burkean attitude toward institutions and military manpower decisions. I would also like to see more people who think like Sun Tzu did in the game with respect to weapon systems and force-structuring planning. I do not object to analysis having some role, and I do not object to people who practice analysis being part of the decision-making process. I just want them to stop being both the players and the referees—both counsels for the plaintiff and court clerks. That is my major complaint.

James L. George, House Committee on Government Operations: Since the subject is the navy, I would like to change the subject and talk about ships. In your prepared remarks, you said we need many more ships. Then you mentioned the case of the *Midway*, which has changed missions six or eight times. The reason *Midway* was able to shift missions, you said, was because it is a large ship, and it could accommodate changes. You also said that surface ships could not do that. I would disagree with that. The World War II cruisers were very flexible because they were large ships.

If you look at the ships that we are about to build in the next five years, you are not seeing larger, more capable ships, but smaller less capable ships. A smaller, very less capable aircraft carrier is being mentioned. The new class of destroyer being talked about—DDX—is going to be a smaller destroyer than DD963. The Trident and its class of submarines are probably going to be replaced with less capable, slower, smaller, submarines. It is all down the line—smaller, less capable.

Flip over to the Soviets, and you see the opposite. They are starting to build larger aircraft carriers, if the intelligence is correct. They are building three classes of cruisers. They are building larger, more capable amphibious ships, but we are not doing amphibious ships at all. They have got a new, more capable submarine, the *Alpha* class.

So I have a three-part question. First, I would like to get your comments on the trends in American shipbuilding; second, your comments on the trends in Soviet shipbuilding; and third, in the light of these trends, your comments on whether something is obviously wrong.

MR. WOOLSEY: Excellent question. First of all, your characterization of trends in both American and Soviet shipbuilding is largely correct, insofar as you were talking about size. Most of the discussion and most of the inclination now with respect to destroyer size is for the United States to go down to a DDX. Most of the discussion about newer carriers has been pointed toward smaller ones, perhaps carrying vertical/short take off and landing (V/STOL) aircraft. It is also true that the Soviets are building larger ones.

In my judgment, size is not as important as design, and I would submit that the primary reason *Midway* has been so successful in changing her mission is not so much that she is large—although she had to be large enough to carry fixed-wing aircraft and jet fixed-wing aircraft when those came along—but rather that she is an aircraft carrier. In spite of what you say about the flexibility of large cruisers, yes, they have been able to change to some extent, but with nowhere near the success of the aircraft carriers. The navy can put high-performance jet aircraft on a *Midway*, but it cannot outfit the 1950s-era cruiser with a very modern air-defense suite without ripping out almost everything and starting over. It would have to start over with the electronics, with the launchers, with the magazines, with almost everything.

The point is, yes, size does provide some flexibility, but it also tends to add cost—a great deal of cost. We want as much size as we really need, but the main thing we need is to start designing other ships and other weapons platforms to carry different sensors and weapons and to be able to change their sensors and weapons as readily as aircraft carriers have been able to change suites of aircraft. To me, that is the pertinent reform, and I would be willing to see slightly smaller American ships, whether destroyers or carriers, if those ships were able to be modernized at a much, much faster rate. But it is true that in general, we have begun to point toward smaller ships, and the Soviets have moved toward larger ones.

MR. PRANGER: We want to thank you, Jim, for enduring the slings and arrows and also for some excellent questions.

MR. WOOLSEY: Thank you.